For God so loved the world that he gave his one and only Son, that whoever believes in him shall not perish but have eternal life. For God did not send his Son into the world to condemn the world, but to save the world through him.
– John 3:16-17 (NIV)

For Bulk Order requests email: contact@adventuresofpookie.com

Printed in the United States of America
Paperback ISBN : 979-8-9877143-9-3

www.AdventuresOfPookie.com

God's Unending Love

Verse

"For I am convinced that neither death nor life, neither angels nor demons, neither the present nor the future, nor any powers, neither height nor depth, nor anything else in all creation, will be able to separate us from the love of God that is in Christ Jesus our Lord." – Romans 8:38-39 (NIV)

Devotional

Have you ever felt scared or worried? Maybe you were nervous about a test at school or worried about a friend. During these times, it's easy to feel alone, but God wants you to know that you are never truly alone.

God's love for you is so big that nothing can separate you from it. Just like a parent or a good friend, God is always with you, cheering you on and holding you close. Whether you're happy, sad, scared, or excited, God loves you the same.

Imagine a warm, cozy blanket that wraps around you on a cold day. That's what God's love is like! It surrounds you and keeps you safe and warm, no matter what happens. And just like you trust that blanket to keep you warm, you can trust God's love to be with you always.

Prayer

Dear God,
Thank you for loving me no matter what. Help me to remember that You are always with me, even when I feel scared or alone. Thank You for Your unending love and for being my forever friend.
In Jesus' name, Amen.

Activity

Draw a picture of something that makes you feel safe and loved. It could be a family member, a pet, or even your favorite place. Remember that God's love is even greater than these things, and it will always be with you.

Trusting in God

Verse

"Trust in the Lord with all your heart and lean not
on your own understanding; in all your ways submit
to Him, and He will make your paths straight."
– Proverbs 3:5-6 (NIV)

Devotional

Sometimes, life can feel like a big maze. We might
not know which way to turn or what the right
choice is. But guess what? We don't have to figure it
out all on our own. God is like the perfect guide who
knows the way through every twist and turn.

When we trust in God with all our hearts, we're
saying, "God, I believe You know what's best for me."
Even when things don't make sense, we can rely on
Him. He promises to help us find the right path if we
listen to Him and follow His ways.

Prayer

Dear God,
Help me to trust You with all my heart. Guide me
in Your ways and help me to lean on You, especially
when I don't understand what's happening. Thank
You for always being there to lead me.
In Jesus' name, Amen.

Activity

As you try to find your way through the maze, remember that just like the lines on the paper, God's guidance helps us navigate life's challenges.

Me

God's Plan

Shining God's Light

Verse

"In the same way, let your light shine before others, that they may see your good deeds and glorify your Father in heaven." – Matthew 5:16 (NIV)

Devotional

Have you ever seen how a small light can brighten up a dark room? You, too, can be like that little light! God has put His light inside of you so that you can shine and bring joy and hope to those around you.

When you do kind things, speak loving words, and help others, you are letting God's light shine through you. This light not only helps others but also shows them how amazing God is. It's like being a lighthouse that guides ships safely to shore.

Prayer

Dear God,
Thank You for putting Your light inside of me. Help me to shine brightly by doing good deeds and showing Your love to everyone I meet. Let others see Your goodness through my actions.
In Jesus' name, Amen.

Activity

Make a list of three kind things you can do for someone today. It could be helping a friend with homework, saying something nice to a family member, or sharing a toy with a sibling. Each time you do something on your list, know that you are shining God's light.

God's Wonderful Creation

Verse

"In the beginning God created the heavens and the earth." — Genesis 1:1 (NIV)

Devotional

Have you ever looked at the stars at night or watched a butterfly flutter by? All of these beautiful things are part of God's amazing creation. From the tallest mountains to the tiniest ants, God made everything with care and love.

God's creation shows us just how powerful and creative He is. It also reminds us that if God took such great care to create the world, He also cares deeply about us. We are His special creation, made in His image, and He loves us very much.

Prayer

Dear God,
Thank You for the beautiful world You created. Help me to see Your greatness in everything around me. Thank You for making me and for loving me.
In Jesus' name, Amen.

Activity

Go on a nature walk with a family member or friend. Look for different things that God has created, like flowers, trees, animals, and clouds. As you walk, think about how each thing you see shows God's creativity and love.

Write or draw one thing that you have seen from your walk that you think best shows God's creativity and love.

God's Strength in Us

Verse
"I can do all this through Him who gives me strength." – Philippians 4:13 (NIV)

Devotional
Have you ever faced a challenge that seemed too big to handle? Maybe it was learning something new or standing up to a bully. It can be scary, but the good news is that you are never alone. God gives you strength to face any challenge.

When you rely on God, He gives you the power to do things you never thought you could. It's like having a superhero's strength inside of you! So, next time you face something hard, remember that God is with you, giving you all the strength you need.

Prayer
Dear God,
Thank You for giving me strength. Help me to remember that I can do all things through You. Be with me in tough times and help me to rely on Your power.
In Jesus' name, Amen.

Activity

Think of a challenge you are facing right now. Write it down in the heart below. This heart represents God's strength surrounding you. Keep this paper where you can see it to remind you that God is with you.

Being Thankful

Verse

"Give thanks in all circumstances; for this is God's will for you in Christ Jesus." – 1 Thessalonians 5:18 (NIV)

Devotional

Sometimes it's easy to forget to say "thank you," especially when things aren't going our way. But God wants us to have thankful hearts all the time. Being thankful helps us to remember all the good things God has done for us.

When we thank God, we show Him that we trust Him and appreciate His blessings. Even in difficult times, we can find something to be thankful for. It could be a friend, a family member, or even a beautiful sunny day.

Prayer

Dear God,
Thank You for all the good things in my life. Help me to remember to be thankful, even when things are tough. Thank You for always being with me and for loving me so much.
In Jesus' name, Amen.

Activity

Create a "Thankfulness Jar." Find a jar and some small pieces of paper. Each day, write down one thing you are thankful for and put it in the jar. Watch as the jar fills up with all the blessings in your life!

Write down a few things in the hearts below to get you started!

Additional Fun: On New Year's Eve, open your jar and read everything that you were thankful for this year. It will help remind us going into the new year what we have to be thankful for.

Loving Others

Verse

"Dear friends, let us love one another, for love comes from God. Everyone who loves has been born of God and knows God." – I John 4:7 (NIV)

Devotional

God is love, and He wants us to share His love with others. When we love others, we are showing them what God is like. This can be as simple as being kind, helping someone in need, or sharing a smile.

Loving others isn't always easy. Sometimes people can be mean or difficult. But God asks us to love everyone, just as He loves us. When we show love, we are spreading God's light and making the world a better place.

Prayer

Dear God,
Help me to love others the way You love me. Show me how to be kind and caring, even when it's hard. Thank You for Your perfect love.
In Jesus' name, Amen.

Activity

Think of someone who needs a little extra love today. Maybe it's a classmate who is often alone or a family member who had a bad day. Do something special for them, like drawing a picture, giving a hug, or simply saying something kind.

Write the name of the person below, then brainstorm some ways you can show them extra love.

Name

Brainstorm...

God Hears Our Prayers

Verse

"This is the confidence we have in approaching God: that if we ask anything according to His will, He hears us." — 1 John 5:14 (NIV)

Devotional

Isn't it amazing to know that God, the Creator of the universe, listens when we talk to Him? When we pray, God hears us. He loves it when we come to Him with our thoughts, worries, and joys.

Prayer is like talking to a close friend. We can tell God anything, and He promises to listen. Sometimes the answer might not be what we expect, but we can trust that God knows what's best for us.

Prayer

Dear God,
Thank You for listening to my prayers.
Help me to remember that
I can talk to You about
anything. Thank You for
always being there
for me.
In Jesus' name,
Amen.

Activity

Start a prayer journal. Each day, write down a prayer to God. It could be something you're thankful for, something you're worried about, or something you need help with. Look back at your prayers to see how God has answered them.

Use the paper below to start.

God's Forgiveness

Verse

"If we confess our sins, He is faithful and just and will forgive us our sins and purify us from all unrighteousness." – I John 1:9 (NIV)

Devotional

Everyone makes mistakes. Sometimes we do things that we know are wrong and feel bad about it. But God is always ready to forgive us when we come to Him and say we're sorry. His forgiveness is a wonderful gift that cleans our hearts and makes us new.

When we confess our sins to God, He promises to forgive us and help us do better next time. This doesn't mean we won't make mistakes again, but it means we can always come back to God and receive His love and forgiveness.

Prayer

Dear God,
Thank You for Your forgiveness.
I am sorry for the things I have done wrong. Please help me to make better choices and to follow You more closely.
Thank You for always loving me.
In Jesus' name, Amen.

Activity

With a pencil, write down or draw pictures of things you feel sorry for or mistakes you have made. Take your eraser and gently erase each word or drawing. As you do, think about how God forgives you and wipes away your mistakes.

After erasing, write or draw something positive and good that you can do instead. This represents a fresh start and a new beginning, just like God gives us when He forgives us.

God's Promises

Verse

"For no matter how many promises God has made, they are 'Yes' in Christ. And so through Him the 'Amen' is spoken by us to the glory of God." – 2 Corinthians 1:20 (NIV)

Devotional

God has made many promises in the Bible, and He always keeps them. When God promises something, we can trust that it will happen because God never breaks His promises. Whether it's His promise to love us, to be with us, or to help us, we can count on Him.

When we read the Bible, we find all kinds of wonderful promises from God. These promises help us feel safe and loved, knowing that God is always looking out for us.

Prayer

Dear God,
Thank You for Your wonderful promises. Help me to remember them and trust in You. Thank You for always keeping Your word.
In Jesus' name, Amen.

Activity

Make a "Promise Page." Write down some of God's promises from the Bible. Decorate the page with drawings or stickers. When you feel worried or sad, look at your Promise Page and remember that God always keeps His promises.

God's Creation is Good

Verse
"God saw all that He had made, and it was very good." — Genesis 1:31 (NIV)

Devotional
When God created the world, He made everything good. From the mountains to the oceans, from the animals to the stars, everything God made is beautiful and wonderful. And that includes you! God made you wonderfully and with great care.

We can see God's goodness in the world around us. When we take time to appreciate His creation, we can see His love and creativity everywhere. Let's take care of God's creation and thank Him for making such an amazing world.

Prayer
Dear God,
Thank You for making such a beautiful world. Help me to see Your goodness in everything around me and to take care of Your creation.
In Jesus' name, Amen.

Activity

There are many ways we can help take care of God's Creation. Write down three things that you can do this week to make sure that our world that God created can stay good. Then, make a plan on how you can do those things.

God's Guidance

Verse

"Your word is a lamp for my feet, a light on my path." – Psalm 119:105 (NIV)

Devotional

Have you ever walked in the dark with a flashlight? The light helps you see where you're going and keeps you from tripping or getting lost. God's Word, the Bible, is like a light for our lives. It helps us know the right way to go and shows us how to live.

When we read the Bible and follow what it says, we are letting God guide us. He shows us the best path and helps us make good choices. Trust God to guide you every day.

Prayer

Dear God,
Thank You for giving us the Bible to guide us. Help me to read it and follow Your ways. Thank You for showing me the right path.
In Jesus' name, Amen.

Activity

Draw a picture of a path with a bright light shining on it. On the path, write words like "kindness," "honesty," and "love" to represent the ways God guides us through His Word.

Jesus Our Friend

Verse

"I no longer call you servants, because a servant does not know his master's business. Instead, I have called you friends, for everything that I learned from my Father I have made known to you."
— John 15:15 (NIV)

Devotional

Isn't it wonderful to have a good friend? Someone who listens, shares, and cares for you? Jesus calls us His friends! He loves us and wants to be close to us, just like a best friend.

As our friend, Jesus is always there for us. We can talk to Him anytime, and He understands everything we go through. Knowing that Jesus is our friend can bring us great comfort and joy.

Prayer

Dear Jesus,
Thank You for being my friend. Help me to remember that You are always with me and that I can talk to You about anything. Thank You for Your love. Amen.

Activity

Write a letter to Jesus using the page below. Tell Him about your day, your worries, and your joys. Thank Him for being your friend and always being there for you.

Serving Others

Verse

"Each of you should use whatever gift you have received to serve others, as faithful stewards of God's grace in its various forms." — I Peter 4:10 (NIV)

Devotional

God has given each of us special gifts and talents. We can use these gifts to serve others and show them God's love. Serving others doesn't have to be a big thing; it can be as simple as helping a friend, sharing your toys, or making someone smile.

When we serve others, we are being like Jesus, who came to serve and not to be served. Let's look for ways to use our gifts to help those around us.

Prayer

Dear God,
Thank You for giving me special gifts and talents. Help me to use them to serve others and show Your love. Thank You for the joy that comes from helping others. In Jesus' name, Amen.

Activity

Think about a gift or talent you have. Write down one way you can use it to help someone this week. Then, make a plan to do it and see how it brings joy to both you and the person you help.

Trusting God

Verse
"Each of you should use whatever gift you have received to serve others, as faithful stewards of God's grace in its various forms." — I Peter 4:10 (NIV)

Devotional
Sometimes things can be scary, like a big storm or trying something new. It's normal to feel afraid, but we don't have to stay afraid. We can trust God to take care of us. God is always with us, and He promises to help us when we are scared.

When we feel afraid, we can pray and ask God to give us courage and peace. Trusting God means believing that He is bigger than our fears and that He loves us very much.

Prayer
Dear God,
When I am afraid, help me to trust You. Thank You for being with me and for loving me. Give me courage and peace.
In Jesus' name, Amen.

Activity

Draw a picture of something that scares you. Next to it, draw a picture of God holding your hand. Remember that God is always with you and you can trust Him in scary times.

Honesty

Verse

"The Lord detests lying lips, but He delights in people who are trustworthy." – Proverbs 12:22 (NIV)

Devotional

Being honest means telling the truth and being trustworthy. God wants us to be honest because it shows that we respect others and care about doing what is right. When we are honest, people can trust us, and we build strong relationships.

Sometimes it might be tempting to lie to avoid getting in trouble, but God sees everything and He values honesty. Being truthful, even when it's hard, is the right thing to do.

Prayer

Dear God,
Help me to be honest and trustworthy. Give me the courage to always tell the truth. Thank You for being a God who loves honesty.
In Jesus' name, Amen.

Activity

Think of a time when you were honest even though it was hard. Write about it below and how it made you feel. Remember that God is pleased when we choose honesty.

A time I was honest...

How it made me feel...

God's Peace

Verse

"Peace I leave with you; my peace I give you. I do not give to you as the world gives. Do not let your hearts be troubled and do not be afraid."
– John 14:27 (NIV)

Devotional

Life can sometimes feel busy and stressful, but God offers us a special kind of peace that calms our hearts. This peace comes from knowing that God is in control and that He cares for us.

When we feel worried or stressed, we can pray and ask God to fill us with His peace. This peace helps us to feel calm and secure, no matter what is happening around us.

Prayer

Dear God,
Thank You for Your peace that calms my heart. Help me to trust You and not be afraid. Fill me with Your peace each day.
In Jesus' name, Amen.

Activity

Find a quiet place and close your eyes. Take a few deep breaths and think about a peaceful scene, like a calm lake or a sunny meadow. Imagine Jesus is there with you, bringing you peace. Write or draw about this scene below.

God's Protection

Verse

"The Lord is my rock, my fortress and my deliverer; my God is my rock, in whom I take refuge."
– Psalm 18:2 (NIV)

Devotional

Have you ever built a sandcastle at the beach? Sometimes, the waves come and wash it away. But imagine a strong, tall castle made of solid rock. Nothing can knock it down! God is like that rock for us. He is our protector and keeps us safe from harm.

When we feel afraid or in danger, we can remember that God is our fortress. We can run to Him and trust that He will take care of us. Just like a rock that doesn't move, God's protection is always there for us.

Prayer

Dear God,
Thank You for being my protector. Help me to remember that You are always with me, keeping me safe. Thank You for being my rock and my fortress.
In Jesus' name, Amen.

Activity

Draw a picture of a strong, tall castle on a rock.
Inside the castle, write your name and decorate it.
Remember that God's protection surrounds you
just like the walls of the castle.

God's Plan for Us

Verse

"For I know the plans I have for you," declares the Lord, "plans to prosper you and not to harm you, plans to give you hope and a future."
— Jeremiah 29:11 (NIV)

Devotional

Sometimes we might wonder what our future will look like. We might worry about what will happen tomorrow or next year. But God has a wonderful plan for each of us! He knows everything about our future and wants what's best for us.

God's plans are full of hope and goodness. Even when we face difficult times, we can trust that God is working things out for our good. He is guiding us each step of the way.

Prayer

Dear God,
Thank You for having a wonderful plan for my life. Help me to trust You and follow Your guidance. Thank You for giving me hope and a bright future. In Jesus' name, Amen.

Activity

Write down three things you dream of doing or becoming in the future. Next to each one, write a short prayer asking God to help you follow His plan for your life.

The Power of Words

Verse
"The tongue has the power of life and death, and those who love it will eat its fruit."
— Proverbs 18:21 (NIV)

Devotional
Have you ever noticed how powerful words can be? Kind words can make someone's day brighter, while mean words can hurt deeply. God wants us to use our words to bring life, encouragement, and love to others.

When we speak kindly and truthfully, we are using our words in a powerful way. We can make a big difference just by saying something nice or encouraging. Let's choose our words wisely and use them to spread God's love.

Prayer
Dear God,
Help me to use my words to bring life and encouragement to others. Teach me to speak kindly and truthfully. Thank You for the power of words and for the chance to make a difference.
In Jesus' name, Amen.

Activity

Make a list of kind words and phrases that you can say to others. Each day, try to say at least one of these kind words to someone. Watch how it brightens their day!

God's Unchanging Love

Verse

"The tongue has the power of life and death, and those who love it will eat its fruit."
– Proverbs 18:21 (NIV)

Devotional

The world around us is always changing. Seasons change, people change, and sometimes our plans change. But there is one thing that never changes: God's love for us. No matter what happens, God's love remains the same.

Jesus is the same yesterday, today, and forever. He loves us just as much today as He did when He walked on Earth. We can always count on His unchanging love to be with us through all of life's changes.

Prayer

Dear Jesus,
Thank You for Your unchanging love. Help me to remember that no matter what happens, You are always the same and Your love for me never changes. Thank You for always being with me.
Amen.

Activity

Draw a heart. Inside the heart, write the words "Jesus' Love." Around the heart, draw pictures of things that change, like seasons, people, and plans. Remember that Jesus' love never changes.

Being a Peacemaker

Verse

"Blessed are the peacemakers, for they will be called children of God." – Matthew 5:9 (NIV)

Devotional

Have you ever seen an argument between friends or family members? It can make everyone feel sad and upset. God calls us to be peacemakers, people who bring peace and help others get along.

Being a peacemaker means showing kindness, listening to others, and helping to solve problems. When we bring peace, we are showing God's love and making the world a better place.

Prayer

Dear God,
Help me to be a peacemaker. Show me how to bring peace and kindness to the people around me. Thank You for the blessing of being called Your child.
In Jesus' name, Amen.

Activity

Think of a time when you helped make peace or saw someone else being a peacemaker. Write about it in your notebook. Then, draw a picture of what being a peacemaker looks like to you.

The Beauty of Forgiveness

Verse

"Be kind and compassionate to one another, forgiving each other, just as in Christ God forgave you." – Ephesians 4:32 (NIV)

Devotional

Have you ever felt hurt by something someone said or did? It can be hard to forgive, but God asks us to forgive others just as He has forgiven us. Forgiveness is a beautiful gift we can give, both to others and ourselves. It helps heal our hearts and brings us closer to God.

When we forgive, we are showing God's love and grace. It doesn't mean we forget what happened, but it means we let go of the hurt and choose to love instead. Forgiveness brings peace and joy to everyone involved.

Prayer

Dear God,
Thank You for forgiving me. Help me to forgive others and show them Your love and grace. Give me the strength to let go of hurt and choose forgiveness.
In Jesus' name, Amen.

Activity

Think of someone you need to forgive. Write their name in the heart below. Pray for that person and ask God to help you forgive them. When you're ready, erase their name, symbolizing that you've let go of the hurt.

God's Wonderful Creation

Verse
"In the beginning God created the heavens and the earth." — Genesis 1:1 (NIV)

Devotional
Take a moment to look around at the world God created. The trees, the sky, the animals, and even you! Everything God made is wonderful and amazing. God took great care in creating the world and everything in it, including you.

When we appreciate God's creation, we see His power and love. Each part of creation reflects God's glory and creativity. Let's take time to enjoy and take care of the beautiful world God has given us.

Prayer
Dear God,
Thank You for creating such a beautiful world. Help me to see Your glory in everything around me and to take care of Your creation. Thank You for making me wonderfully.
In Jesus' name, Amen.

Activity

Think of something in nature that amazes you. Draw a picture of it below and write a sentence thanking God for creating it.

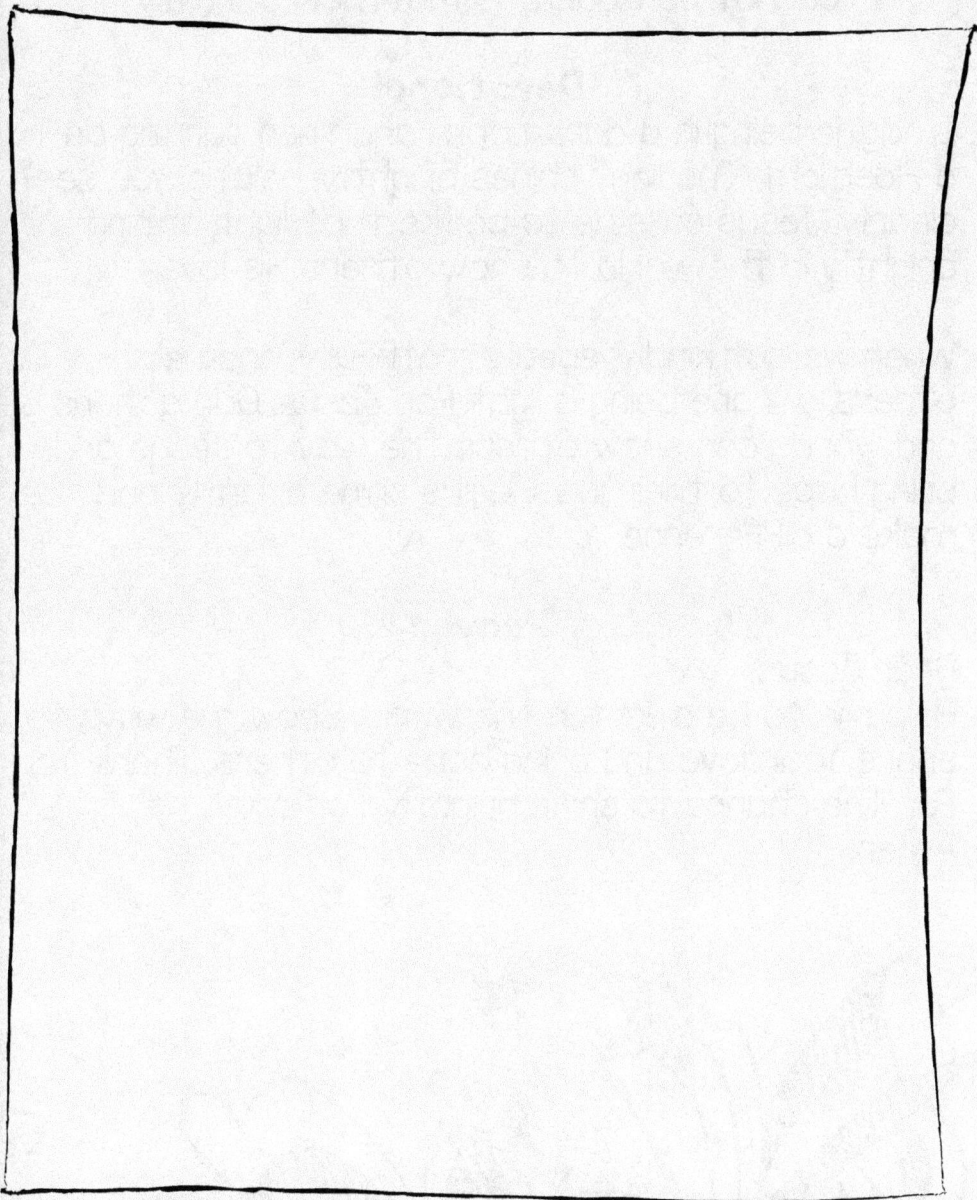

Being a Light for Jesus

Verse
"You are the light of the world. A town built on a hill cannot be hidden." – Matthew 5:14 (NIV)

Devotional
Imagine being in a dark room and then turning on a flashlight. The light shines brightly, helping you see clearly. Jesus calls us to be like that light, shining brightly in the world to show others His love.

When we act kindly, speak truthfully, and help others, we are being a light for Jesus. Our actions and words can show others the way to Jesus and bring hope to their lives. Let's shine brightly and make a difference.

Prayer
Dear Jesus,
Help me to be a light in the world. Show me ways to share Your love and bring hope to others. Thank You for the chance to shine brightly for You.
Amen.

Activity

Draw a picture of a lighthouse shining its light. Inside the light, write or draw ways you can show Jesus' love to others. Remember that even small acts of kindness can shine brightly.

Patience in God's Timing

Verse

"There is a time for everything, and a season for every activity under the heavens."
– Ecclesiastes 3:1 (NIV)

Devotional

Have you ever had to wait for something you really wanted? Waiting can be hard, but God has a perfect timing for everything. Just like flowers bloom in their season, God's plans for us happen at the right time.

When we trust God's timing, we learn patience and faith. God knows what's best for us and when it's best for us. Even when waiting is hard, we can trust that God's plans are always good.

Prayer

Dear God,
Thank You for Your perfect timing.
Help me to be patient and
trust in Your plans for me.
Thank You for knowing
what's best for me
and when it's best.
In Jesus' name, Amen.

Activity

Draw a picture of a flower growing. Write the words "God's Timing" above it. Remember that just like the flower, good things happen in God's perfect time.

God's Everlasting Love

Verse

"Give thanks to the Lord, for He is good; His love endures forever." — Psalm 136:1 (NIV)

Devotional

God's love for us never ends. It's like a river that keeps flowing or a sunrise that happens every morning. No matter what we do or where we go, God's love is always with us. It's a love that never fails and never gives up.

Knowing that God loves us forever gives us comfort and joy. We can face each day with confidence, knowing that we are deeply loved by God. Let's give thanks for His everlasting love and share it with others.

Prayer

Dear God,
Thank You for Your everlasting love. Help me to remember that Your love never ends and that I am always loved by You. Thank You for being so good to me.
In Jesus' name, Amen.

Activity

Get 8 strips of paper about one inch wide and six to eight inches long. Can use colorful paper for extra fun or color each strip as you go.

On each strip of paper, write something that shows God's love or a way you can share God's love with others. For example, "God loves me no matter what," "Help a friend," or "Say kind words."

After writing on the strips, loop one strip to form a circle and glue or tape the ends together. Take another strip, loop it through the first circle to form another circle, and glue or tape the ends together. Continue this process, creating a chain of love.

As you add each strip to the chain, say a prayer thanking God for His everlasting love or asking Him to help you share His love with others.

Hang your love chain in a place where you can see it every day. Each link in the chain will remind you of God's endless love and the ways you can share it with others.

Jesus' Love on the Cross

Verse

"But God demonstrates His own love for us in this: While we were still sinners, Christ died for us."
— Romans 5:8 (NIV)

Devotional

Have you ever wondered how much Jesus loves you? The best way to understand His incredible love is to think about what He did on the cross. Jesus came to Earth to show us God's love, and the greatest example of this love was when He died on the cross for our sins.

Jesus didn't have to die; He chose to because He loves us so much. By dying on the cross, Jesus took the punishment for all the wrong things we've done so that we can be forgiven and have a close relationship with God. His love is so big that He was willing to give up everything for us.

When we think about Jesus on the cross, we remember how much He loves us and how we can love others in return. His love is powerful and never-ending, and it changes our hearts and lives.

Prayer

Dear Jesus,
Thank You for loving me so much that You died on the cross for my sins. Help me to understand Your great love and to share it with others. Thank You for forgiving me and giving me new life. Amen.

Activity

On the cross, write "Jesus Loves Me" in the center. Around the cross, draw or write words and pictures that remind you of Jesus' love. This could include hearts, kind actions, forgiving, praying, helping others, etc. Decorate the cross with colors and designs that make you think of love and Jesus' sacrifice.

About the Author

Rebecca graduated from Malone College in 2008 with a Bachelor's degree in Youth Ministry. She started writing & illustrating in 2013, about her dog Pookie, when she wanted a fun and wholesome story for her nieces and nephews, some of which were learning to read. She plans to keep up her series and write others. In 2019, she launched a publishing and entertainment company to help kids explore and nurture their creative side through books, tv shows, and art classes.

Along with The Adventures of Pookie children's book series, she is the illustrator of her sister, Megan Yee's books in the God's Books series. She is also the author of the personal development book *The Creative Minds Guide to Success*. She travels full time in a 5th wheel RV with her husband Eric, and their dog, Bailey, for his job as a Journeyman Lineman and writes about their adventures along the way.

For free printables, visit
AdventuresOfPookie.com

The Adventures of
Pookie LLC

ENTERTAINMENT

Books   **Shows**   **Classes**

Scan the code to go to our YouTube page to see all of our tv shows, movies, and art classes, including our new Fearless Faith cartoons and Mission Fat Hearts the Movie.